KINDERGARTEN COUNT TO 100

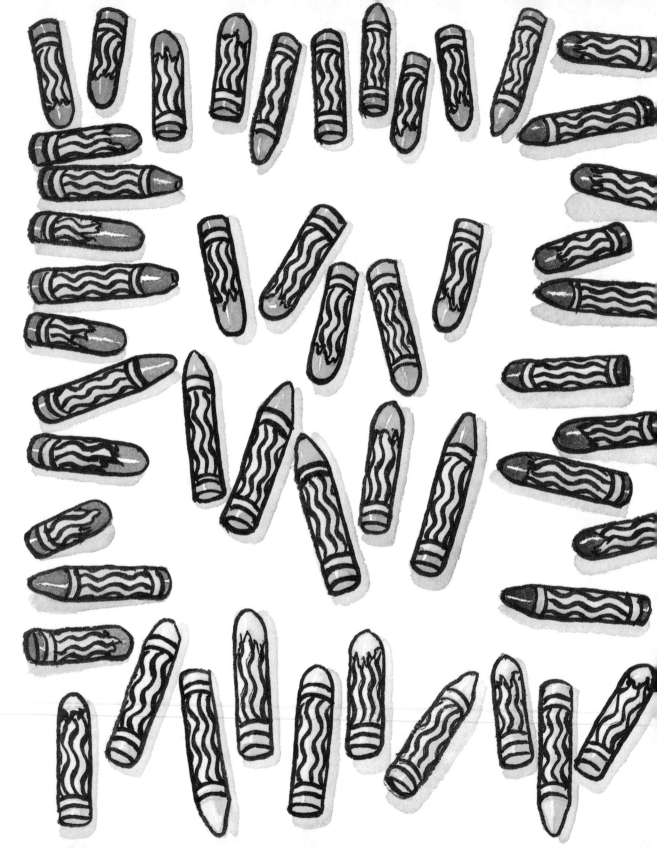

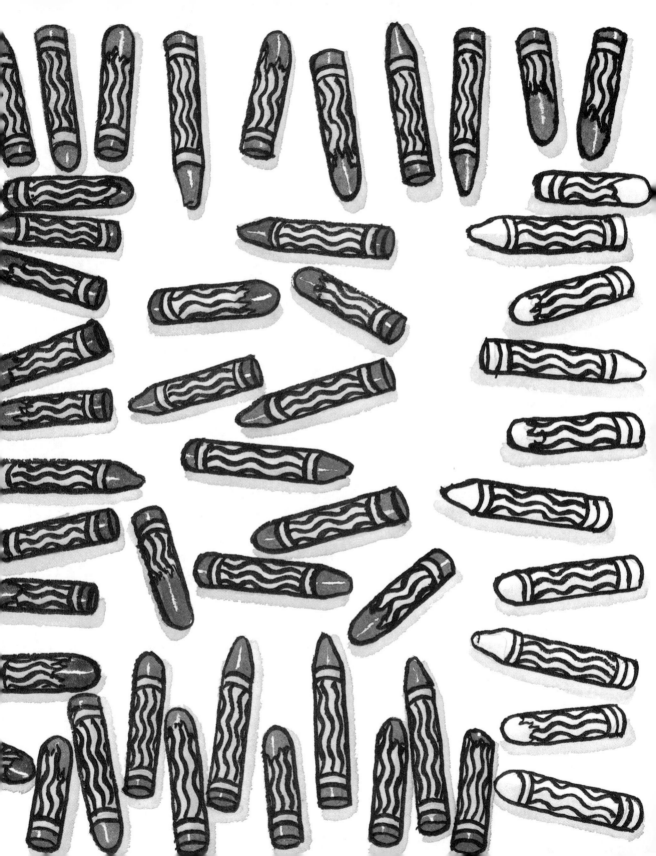

This book is dedicated to my
sixth-grade teacher, Joan Chandler,
with deep thanks.

A special thanks to my kindergarten coaches,
Jane Conte and Nancy Hammell.
—J.R.

ISBN 0-439-79957-0

12 11 10 9 8 7   8 9 10/0

Printed in the U.S.A.   23

First Scholastic paperback printing, September 2005

KINDERGARTEN COUNT TO 100

BY JACQUELINE ROGERS

SCHOLASTIC INC.
Cartwheel B·O·O·K·S

New York   Toronto   London   Auckland   Sydney
Mexico City   New Delhi   Hong Kong   Buenos Aires

"Wake up! Wake up!"
I shout down the hall.

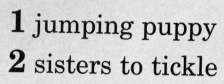

1 jumping puppy
2 sisters to tickle

3 eating breakfast

4 lunches to pack

Race to the bus!

5 friends with baseball caps

I check out my lunch.
6 things in my bag . . .

1. a juice box
2. a sandwich
3. a bag of chips
4. a napkin
5. a cupcake
6. and a note from my mom

Inside the school now,
I walk to my room.

It takes **7** giant steps
from the fountain to my door...

...and **8** easy steps to my cubby.

Hey, there's Matthew.
"I like your haircut!"

It's our time to play.
I love to color!
Blue is my favorite,
then purple,
then green.

9 crayons in all—
YOU name the colors!

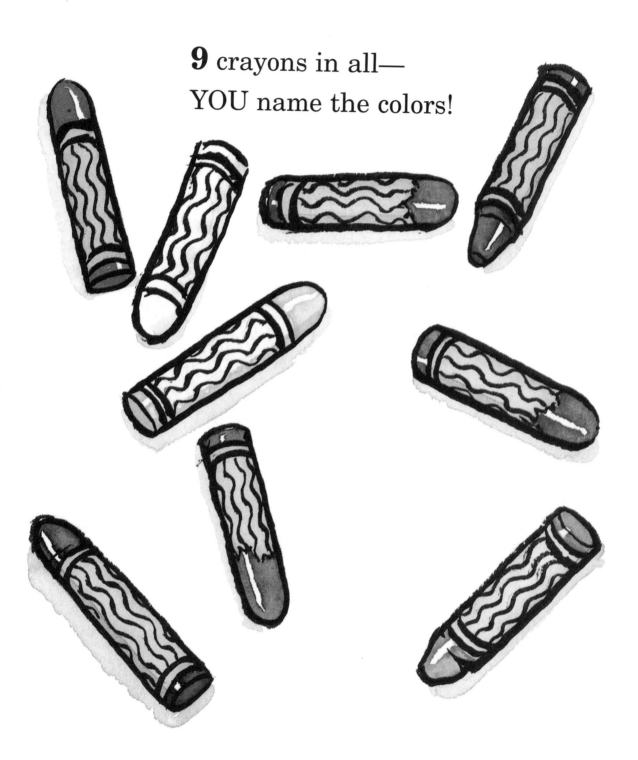

Cleanup time now,
then salute to the flag.

Let's do the calendar!

10 days gone by in this month.

This is the tenth day of the month.

Sunday	Monday	Tuesday	Wednesday	Thursday	Friday	Saturday
			1	2	3	4
5	6	7	8	9	10	11
12	13	14	15	16	17	18
19	20	21	22	23	24	25
26	27	28	29	30	31	

We made a castle
with **100** paper cups!

There are **11** puppies
in the picture.

There are **12** d's
on my paper.

After lunch, it's time to go out.

13 leaps to the slide.

Wow! That's a fast one! Let's do it again!

Back for
Show-and-Tell.
It's Calley's turn first.

My granny knit this sweater for me.

Peter is second.

I found these feathers in the woods behind my house.

This is my puppet, Harold. He can talk. Say 'Hi,' Harold.

Hi!

Jillian is third.

It's MY TURN! It's MY TURN!
I show them my set of
14 shiny cars and trucks.

It's math time now,
15 bright-colored cards.

I pick **8** bears.
Matthew picks **8** bears.
That's **16** altogether.

Clean up, then off to my favorite...
GYM!
Big balls and little balls,
17 in all.

Snack time,
then pack up our stuff.

18 of us line up,
19 counting Mrs. Gardener.

Good-bye! Good-bye!
20 waving hands.

Count **100** steps off these pages.... Go!

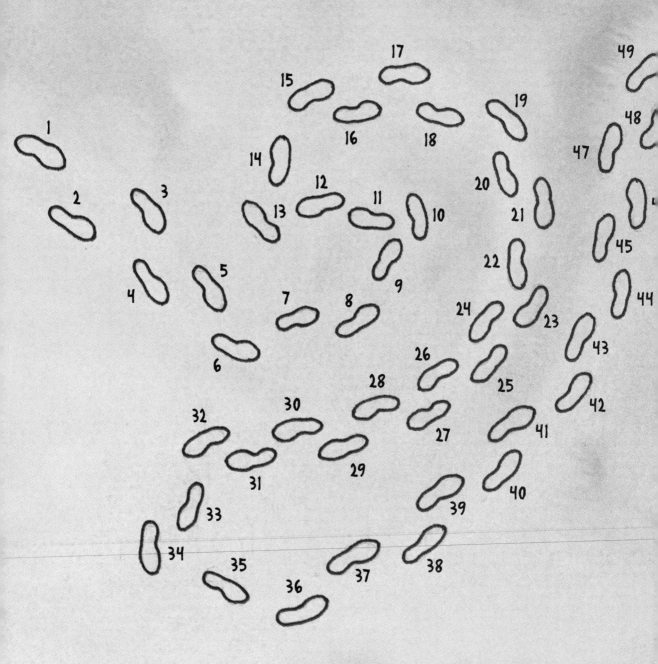